THE FACTS

About Election and Voter Fraud

Naomi Rockler

San Diego, CA

For more information, contact:
ReferencePoint Press, Inc.
PO Box 27779
San Diego, CA 92198
www.ReferencePointPress.com

LIBRARY OF CONGRESS CATALOGING-IN-PUBLICATION DATA

Names: Rockler, Naomi, author.
Title: The facts about election and voter fraud / by Naomi Rockler.
Description: San Diego, CA : ReferencePoint Press, Inc., 2024. | Includes
  bibliographical references and index.
Identifiers: LCCN 2023040300 (print) | LCCN 2023040301 (ebook) | ISBN
  9781678207342 (library binding) | ISBN 9781678207359 (ebook)
Subjects: LCSH: Elections--Corrupt practices--United States. | Political
  corruption--United States--Juvenile literature. | Voting--United
  States--Juvenile literature. | United States--Politics and government.
Classification: LCC JK1994 .R64 2024 (print) | LCC JK1994 (ebook) | DDC
  324.973--dc23/eng/20230912
LC record available at https://lccn.loc.gov/2023040300
LC ebook record available at https://lccn.loc.gov/2023040301

CONTENTS

A Real but Rare Problem

During a 2021 statewide election in Georgia, a ballot was mistakenly sent to a woman's previous address. The new person at that address, William Chase, decided this was an opportunity to vote twice. He forged the woman's signature and mailed in the ballot. Then he voted again, using his own ballot. Chase was caught when the woman reported the missing ballot, and investigators found Chase's fingerprints on the ballot he sent in. Voting more than once and forging someone's signature on a ballot are examples of voter fraud, which is a crime. Chase was sentenced to twenty-five years in prison.

The freedom for people to elect their own leaders is a requirement in a democratic society. Any fraudulent action aimed at altering the outcome of an election is a threat to democracy. "The integrity of elections that are free of fraud and secure is one of the things America is founded on," explains Georgia secretary of state Brad Raffensperger. "We protect them vigorously and prosecute people who undermine them just as vigorously."[1]

Although voter fraud is serious, it is also extremely rare. Over 4 million people voted during this Georgia election, and the Chase case was the only documented instance of fraud. "Voter fraud is virtually non-existent," says George Christenson, a Wisconsin election clerk. "I would have to venture a guess that's about the same odds as getting hit by lightning."[2]

What Are Voter Fraud and Election Fraud?

The terms *voter fraud* and *election fraud* are often used interchangeably. Typically, voter fraud refers to an individual's attempt to vote illegally. Election fraud usually refers to election officials tampering with votes or manipulating election results.

An example of voter fraud is voter impersonation. This includes pretending to be someone else at a polling place—like a person who has died—or marking another person's ballot and representing it as one's own. Another example of voter fraud is voter registration fraud. This occurs when someone who is not eligible to vote registers anyway or registers under a false name.

Examples of election fraud include destroying or miscounting ballots in order to impact the election count, as well as tampering with voting machines. Paying people to vote for a specific candidate is also election fraud.

How Common Is Voter Fraud?

Voter and election fraud do exist. The Heritage Foundation, a conservative think tank, maintains a database of documented cases of voter fraud. It reported over fourteen hundred voter fraud cases from 1982 to 2023. "The mounting collection of cases continue to disprove the narrative that voter fraud is not real,"[3] argue Katie Samalis-Aldrich and Hans A. von Spakovsky of the Heritage Foundation.

In addition to showing that voter fraud is real, the database reveals that it is rare. Those fourteen hundred cases represent a fraction of the billions of votes cast during that forty-one-year period. "Fraud does occur but on a very infinitesimal basis," says Tammy Patrick, a prominent US elections expert. "When we talk about fraud by mail or in-person voting, the real debates are how many zeroes after the decimal before you get to a number, out of tens of millions if not hundreds of millions of ballots cast over years."[4]

Election systems are designed with built-in safeguards to prevent fraud. These safeguards are by and large successful. "There is a very specific reason why we don't see many

—Amber McReynolds, election security expert

instances of fraud, and that is because the system is designed to catch it, to flag it and then hold those people accountable,"[5] says election security expert Amber McReynolds. These measures include keeping careful inventory of ballots, backing up voting machine tallies with paper trails, and sealing ballot boxes to prevent tampering.

Nonetheless, many Americans believe voter fraud is widespread. According to a 2022 Gallup poll, only 63 percent of Americans were confident that the upcoming election results would be accurate and not impacted by fraud.

A person puts mail-in ballots in a mailbox in San Diego, California, in 2020. Voter fraud—either by mail or in person—is a crime, but it is also very rare.

A Polarizing Issue

Polls show that Republicans are significantly more concerned than Democrats about voter and election fraud. According to a 2023 AP-NORC poll, 71 percent of Democrats are highly confident that the 2024 election votes will be counted accurately, but only 22 percent of Republicans share this confidence.

One reason for this disparity is former president Donald Trump's repeated assertions that he lost the 2020 presidential election because of fraud. Many Republicans believe Trump. According to a 2023 Monmouth University poll, 68 percent of Republicans said that Trump only lost because of voter fraud.

Echoing these concerns, many states have passed new voting laws. These laws include restrictions on mail-in ballots and on the types of identification that must be provided before someone can vote. Supporters of these laws argue that they are needed to protect free and fair elections. Opponents argue that these laws are unnecessary because voter fraud is not widespread—and because some of these laws make it harder for eligible people to vote.

Many Americans—including legislators—overestimate how common voter and election fraud are. This overestimation has resulted in laws that sometimes create unnecessary obstacles to voting. To prevent this, Americans need an accurate understanding of how much voter fraud actually exists, how it occurs, and whether measures already in place have kept it from becoming widespread or whether new measures are needed.

CHAPTER ONE

Registering to Vote

In 2021 Jordan Daniels and Devin King worked in Florida for a third-party voter registration organization—an organization that helps people register to vote. The two men received bonuses if they registered a certain number of people. To earn more money, Daniels and King created fake voter registrations for dead people and used living people's personal information to register them without their knowledge. Authorities are not sure how they obtained this information. Even so, the two were caught when county officials noticed abnormalities on the applications. Both were convicted in 2022 of criminal use of personal information. Daniels received a ten-month prison sentence. King was sentenced to one year in prison.

This is a case of voter registration fraud, a crime in which people falsify the voter registration information of themselves or others for personal or political gain. The state of Florida took note. In May 2023 Florida passed a law that made it significantly more difficult for third-party organizations to register voters.

Supporters of this law argue it is necessary to ensure that organizations do not misuse or mishandle sensitive voter information. However, opponents argue it is unnecessary because voter registration fraud cases are uncommon—and that the benefit of helping people register greatly outweighs the minor risk of voter fraud. "Nonpartisan third-party voter registration organizations have worked in Florida for years, helping our neighbors join the democratic process by getting them onto the voter rolls and involved in their government,"[6] says Florida House Democratic leader Fentrice Driskell.

Florida is not the only state that recently passed new laws for the purpose of preventing voter registration fraud. Similar laws that restrict third-party voter registration organizations were passed in Kansas in 2021 and Missouri in 2022. Since 2021 many states—including Arizona, Idaho, and Mississippi—have passed stricter requirements for the identification voters need to provide when registering to vote. This includes proof of citizenship and a photo ID.

Supporters of these laws say that voter registration fraud is a serious enough problem to warrant these types of regulations, even if these laws make it more difficult for some people to register. However, research shows that voter registration fraud is uncommon.

How Does Voter Registration Work?

Although voting is a constitutional right for US citizens who are at least eighteen years old, Americans are not automatically permitted to vote. They have to go through a process called voter registration. The purpose of voter registration is to prevent fraud by establishing that all voters are who they say they are and that they are eligible to vote. "Voter registration is a regular and ongoing process to make sure that our elections are as inclusive, accurate and credible as possible,"[7] explains Lauren Kunis, former director of the National Voter Registration Day program.

In the United States voter registration is decentralized. This means that people register to vote in the county where they live, as opposed to registering with the federal government. To register, people fill out a voter registration application. Then they are added to the local voter roll and can vote in local, state, and national elections.

—Lauren Kunis, former director of the National Voter Registration Day program

Because voting is decentralized, states have different laws that govern voter registration. Although a similar voter registration application is used in all states, states ask for different information on the application. For example, some states require people to include their party affiliation or Social Security number. In some states people have to register before a deadline, and these deadlines vary by state. Twenty-three states have same-day registration, which means that people can register to vote at the polls. In addition, some states require voters to reregister if they have not voted for a set period of time. One state, North Dakota, does not have voter registration at all.

People can register to vote in a number of ways. Because of the 1993 National Voter Registration Act—known as the Motor Voter Act—people can register when they apply for or renew their driver's license. Some states allow people to register online. Oth-

A volunteer at the 2020 Women's March in Philadelphia helps people register to vote. In recent years, many states have passed new laws that make it more difficult for third-party organizations to register voters.

ers require people to mail in an application or register in person at a government office. Some states have automatic voter registration, which means individuals are registered automatically when they interact with government agencies such as the Department of Motor Vehicles, unless they actively decline.

What Is Voter Registration Fraud?

Lying on a voter registration application is considered voter fraud. This includes using a false name—like a fictitious person or the name of a person who has moved or died. People may be motivated to do this in order to vote twice—once with their true identity and once with their false one. Another form of voter registration fraud is lying about one's eligibility. People cannot register to vote if they are not citizens or (in some situations) if they have committed a felony.

It is also fraud to register to vote in a county or a state where one does not live. People may be motivated to do so for political reasons, like if they want to help a candidate in a different county get elected. Registering to vote in multiple locations—or any attempt to register to vote multiple times—is fraud.

Voter registration fraud can also be committed by people other than individual voters. For example, election officials are guilty of fraud if they register someone who is not eligible. In addition, they are guilty of fraud if they enter false information into a person's record so that the person cannot vote, like false information about the voter's criminal record.

How Common Is Voter Registration Fraud?

The Heritage Foundation, which documents proven cases of voter fraud, listed over two hundred instances of voter registration fraud from 1982 to 2023. The majority of these cases involved an ineligible felon registering to vote. For example, in 2022, after felon Charles Skiles of Idaho attempted to register to vote four times, county officials stopped issuing warnings to Skiles and reported him to law enforcement. In other instances, voters registered at a fake address in order to vote illegally in places where they did not live. For example, Lawrence Klug of Wisconsin was convicted in 2022 of claiming that he lived at an address that was actually a local UPS Store. Some cases involved voters registering in multiple locations. For example, in 2023 Zameahia Ismail of Minnesota was convicted for registering to vote twice—once in her own precinct and once in another precinct so she could vote for a specific candidate. Other cases involve registering to vote using the name of a deceased person, like Richard Davis of California, who registered to vote on behalf of his deceased father in 2018. There were also a few instances of voters using fictitious names, including a 2021 case in Montana, where a man registered under the name Miguel Raton—Spanish for Mickey Mouse.

One thing the Heritage Foundation database demonstrates is that by far the majority of voter registration fraud incidents were isolated acts by individual voters. There are very few instances in the database of voter registration fraud by election officials, third-party organizations, hackers, or anyone working as a part of an organized effort to create falsified voter registration applications. In a comprehensive study of fraud in the 2020 election, the Associated Press also reached this conclusion. "Virtually every case

A prospective voter registers online. Registering online is just one of a number of ways that people can register to vote.

was based on an individual acting alone to cast additional ballots,"[8] wrote Christina A. Cassidy of the Associated Press.

The Brennan Center for Justice, a liberal think tank that focuses on voting rights issues, notes that the number of cases of voter registration fraud in the Heritage Foundation database represents a tiny percentage of votes cast over approximately forty years. Moreover, the Brennan Center states, the database does not take into account instances in which ineligible people broke the law unintentionally. This is especially true in the case of felons, as laws about which felons can vote vary by state and can be confusing. For example, in 2022 nineteen felons were arrested for registering to vote in Florida. Because of a Florida law that allowed felons to vote, they thought they had the right to do so. However, the law had recently been amended to exclude some felons, and these nineteen felons were no longer eligible. "The amendment and subsequent actions by state lawmakers caused mass confusion about who was eligible, and the state's voter registration forms offer no clarity,"[9] explains Lawrence Mower of the

Does Automatic Voter Registration Prevent Fraud?

As of June 2023, twenty-three states and the District of Columbia have adopted automatic voter registration. This means that citizens are automatically registered to vote when they interact with a government office—for example, when they renew a driver's license—unless they opt out. Government offices share information about voters with a centralized voter registration database, including the addresses of voters. The system is updated continuously, so if a person moves and fills out a change-of-address form with the post office, that updated information is sent to the database. State information about deaths is also used to update the database. Proponents of automatic registration argue that this system prevents fraud because it keeps the voter rolls up-to-date and accurate. It also eliminates paper voter registration forms, which are vulnerable to clerical errors. In contrast, opponents say this system is too automated. If there is an error in the system—perhaps about someone's eligibility to vote—that error may go unnoticed because no one is physically looking at this information.

Tampa Bay Times. In some cases Florida voting officials—who also were not aware of the amendment—advised felons that they were eligible to vote.

Safeguards to Prevent Voter Registration Fraud

Voter registration fraud is rare in part because of safeguards to prevent it and to catch offenders. One simple safeguard is that voters have to sign their voter registration application. When people vote, they have to provide another signature. Election workers check the signature voters used to register with the one they used to vote, and these signatures need to match. If they do not, voters can only vote with a provisional ballot, which will only be counted after officials investigate further.

Another safeguard is the routine maintenance of state voting rolls, which are lists of registered voters. Election officials update the voting rolls regularly to remove the names of people who have died or moved to a different voting district, or who have become ineligible to vote for some other reason, such as a felony conviction. They also update the list if a voter changes his or her name. Because voter rolls usually have current information about people's addresses, this can prevent people from voting in a place where they do not live. In addition, because states have records of what names were removed from the voter rolls, this prevents people from using these names fraudulently to register to vote.

On an interstate level, an important tool for preventing fraud is the Electronic Registration Information Center, or ERIC. ERIC is in effect a multistate voter roll; it is a nonprofit organization that maintains information about registered voters in all of its member states. As of 2023 twenty-six states and the District of Columbia were members. States submit information about registered voters to ERIC, which also has access to Social Security death records.

ERIC helps prevent voter registration fraud in several ways. For one thing, it can identify people who have registered to vote in multiple states. "While ERIC has confirmed that double voting is rare, with only a few dozen cases of fraud nationwide in a

A voter in Milwaukee, Wisconsin, signs her name in the paper poll book in 2022. One important voter safeguard is that election workers check the signatures voters use to register with the ones they use to vote, and these signatures need to match.

national election, it has helped identify those rarities,"[10] explain journalist Major Garrett and election security expert David Becker. In addition, because ERIC has a more complete set of information than state voter rolls, it is an even better safeguard to catch voters attempting to register under the name of someone who has died or moved.

A new safeguard for preventing voter registration fraud is the Caltech/MIT Voting Technology Project (VTP). This technology uses algorithms to monitor day-to-day changes in a state's voter registration database. If activity occurs that is outside the norm—such as a duplicate record—the VTP flags the activity so it can be investigated. This system is also designed to catch instances of voter roll hacking. The VTP is currently being tested in Southern California, with the hopes of expanding the use of this technology nationwide. "Our vision is to have all states upload voter data on a daily basis and to have algorithms monitor their integrity,"[11] explains computer scientist Michael Alvarez.

Is Voter Registration Fraud a Serious Problem?

When people unlawfully register to vote, it is a problem. How serious a problem is it? One way to answer that is to look at how often it happens. Research shows that it has happened more than two hundred times since the 1980s. These cases include ineligible people registering to vote, people registering to vote multiple times, and third-party election workers creating false voter registration records to earn financial bonuses. Many cases of unlawful registration involved felons who were unaware that they were ineligible to vote. The system has built-in measures to prevent and catch instances of voter registration fraud, including regular maintenance of voter rolls and the interstate sharing of voting data through ERIC. Voter registration fraud exists, but it is not widespread enough to impact election results.

CHAPTER TWO

In-Person Voter Impersonation

In 2020 Ralph Thurman voted in the presidential election at his local polling place in Chester County, Pennsylvania. He asked a poll worker if he could also vote on behalf of his son and was told that he could not because that was illegal. Thurman, however, did not take "no" for an answer. Since Pennsylvania does not require voters to show identification at the polls, he returned later to the polling place wearing a hat and sunglasses and identified himself as Thurman's son. He received a ballot and voted. However, another poll worker recognized Thurman and contacted law enforcement. Thurman pleaded guilty, was sentenced to three years of probation, and was barred from voting for four years.

This is an example of in-person voter impersonation, wherein someone pretends to be another person at the polls and casts a vote. Although Thurman's case sounds like a bad comedy sketch, voter impersonation is a form of election fraud that is taken seriously. It is a crime in every state, and a federal crime if the impersonator casts a vote for a presidential candidate.

The Chester County case is unusual. The number of documented cases of voter impersonation at the polls is small. Even so, many states have recently passed stricter voter identification laws to prevent voter impersonation. Although many people believe that requiring identification of some kind at the polls is reasonable, critics say these laws go too far and make it unnecessarily difficult for Americans to vote.

How Are Voters Identified at the Polls?

When a voter arrives at a polling place, he or she checks in with a poll worker, who has a copy of the local voting roll. If the voter is on the list, he or she receives a ballot and can vote. If the voter is not on the list, he or she can register at the poll if the state has same-day voter registration. If not, and if the voter believes he or she is registered, that voter can cast a provisional ballot. This ballot will be counted if election officials later determine the voter was duly registered at the time.

Most of this works the same in every state, except for one important detail: identification. What proof does the poll worker have that the voter is not impersonating someone else? This depends on the state's voter identification laws. "Voter ID laws serve three core functions," election lawyer J. Christian Adams states. "They are checks against errors, they prevent wrongdoing, and they give citizens confidence in the voting process in general."[12]

Voter ID laws vary widely by state. In some states voters do not have to show identification at all when they vote. Voters simply state their name and address to poll workers, who then confirm that the person appears on the voter roll. In other states vot-

A person shows ID at a polling station. While voter ID is required in some states, in others it is not.

ers have to show identification. This may include a military ID, a student ID, or certain pieces of mail (like a utility bill) with a person's name and address on it. Many states require people to show identification only the first time they vote in that precinct. In other states people cannot vote unless they show a government-issued photo ID, like a driver's license or a passport.

The Voter ID Debate

Some states that used to allow several forms of ID no longer do so. In these states, to obtain a ballot, a voter must show a government-issued photo ID. Supporters of photo ID laws argue that this is the most effective way to prevent people from impersonating someone else at the polls. They argue that although a small percentage of Americans do not have a photo ID, this problem is outweighed by the benefits of preventing voter impersonation. They also point out that in some states with photo ID laws, like Wisconsin and Georgia, the government provides voters with free photo ID voting cards if they need one.

—American Civil Liberties Union

In contrast, opponents of photo voter ID laws argue that they serve as an obstacle that makes it harder for some Americans to vote. A significant number of Americans do not have easy access to this kind of identification. According to the American Civil Liberties Union (ACLU), "About 7% of U.S. citizens—or more than 16 million Americans—cannot confirm that they have a government-issued ID."[13]

Obtaining a photo ID can be time consuming and expensive. For example, according to voter information website Wisevoter, the average price of a driver's license in the United States (which varies by state) is about thirty-four dollars and runs as high as eighty-nine dollars in Washington State. This does not include the cost of obtaining an official copy of a birth certificate from the county of one's birth, which is required to apply for a license. The price of a birth

Do Poll Worker Shortages Increase the Risk of Fraud?

Poll workers serve as a line of defense against potential voter impersonation. They are there to make sure that no one votes unless he or she is on the list. Unfortunately, in recent years there has been a growing shortage of volunteers and paid workers who are willing to staff the polls on Election Day. In a 2022 study, the Brennan Center for Justice reported that about 20 percent of poll workers do not intend to return for the 2024 election. One of the reasons for this is continued concern about exposure to COVID-19. Another is the nationwide trend of harassment and violent threats against poll workers and other election workers, caused largely by fabricated accounts of election workers rigging the election. In addition, many older people who have been working the polls for years are retiring, and their replacements do not share the level of experience and knowledge of their predecessors. It remains to be seen whether there will be a serious shortage of poll workers in the 2024 election and what impact this will have on security.

certificate ranges from nine dollars in Florida to thirty-four dollars in Michigan. The cost of transportation may also be an issue. "The travel required is often a major burden on people with disabilities, the elderly, or those in rural areas without access to a car or public transportation," argues the ACLU. "In Texas, some people in rural areas must travel approximately 170 miles to reach the nearest ID office."[14] Critics of voter ID laws also point out that these laws disproportionately impact people of color. About 13 percent of Black Americans of voting age lack government-issued photo ID, as opposed to only 4 percent of White Americans.

Opponents of photo voter ID laws argue that voter impersonation almost never happens, and therefore photo voter ID laws are unnecessary and do more harm than good. In contrast, supporters of photo voter ID laws argue that voter impersonation is a serious problem, and photos are needed to prevent it. To make an informed judgment about this issue, it is important to understand how often this kind of impersonation occurs.

How Common Is In-Person Voter Impersonation?

Voter ID laws have a good deal of public support. According to a 2022 Gallup poll, eight out of ten Americans agree that voters should show photo identification when they vote in person. This includes 97 percent of Republicans and 53 percent of Democrats. Support for voter ID laws is noteworthy, since most Americans are much less likely to support other voting restrictions, like restrictions on early voting.

However, despite Americans' unusually high level of support for photo voter ID laws as a tool to prevent voter impersonation fraud, this type of fraud is actually less common than other kinds of voting fraud. According to the League of Women Voters, a voting rights organization, "The rate of in-person voter impersonation is extremely low: only 0.00004% of all ballots cast. It's worth noting that this rate is even significantly lower than other rare forms of voter fraud, such as absentee ballot fraud, which voter photo ID laws do not address."[15]

The Heritage Foundation's voter fraud database lists twenty-five instances of someone attempting to obtain a ballot by pretending to be someone else. These cases occurred at polling places from 2004 to 2023. Most involved people trying to obtain the ballot of a deceased relative.

Voter impersonation, when it exists, is almost always the act of individuals. As University of California, Los Angeles, law and political science professor Richard Hasen argues, it is nearly impossible that an organized campaign of voter impersonation could happen on a large enough scale to impact election results. Hasen argues:

> It is an exceedingly dumb way to steal an election because one would have to hire people to go to the polls claiming to be someone else, hope that the people being impersonated had not yet voted, hope that the people being paid to commit felonies would actually cast a secret ballot the way the payer wants, and repeat this process undetected on a large enough scale to sway an election.[16]

Why Is In-Person Voter Impersonation So Rare?

One contributing factor to the low rates of in-person voting fraud is simply the decreasing number of people who vote in person. This is largely due to the COVID-19 pandemic, which began in 2020. To avoid being exposed to the virus, many voters in the 2020 general election chose to vote by mail instead of voting at the polls. According to the US Census Bureau, 46 percent of voters cast their ballots by mail in 2020. While these numbers shrank somewhat in 2022, to 33 percent, that still represented a third of all voters. In contrast, voting by mail used to be much less common. In 2002 only about 14 percent of voters voted by mail.

Perhaps the most significant reason why voter impersonation at the polls is rare is because the election system has built-in safeguards to prevent and catch it. One safeguard is that in every state, voters need to sign a book when they check into the polls.

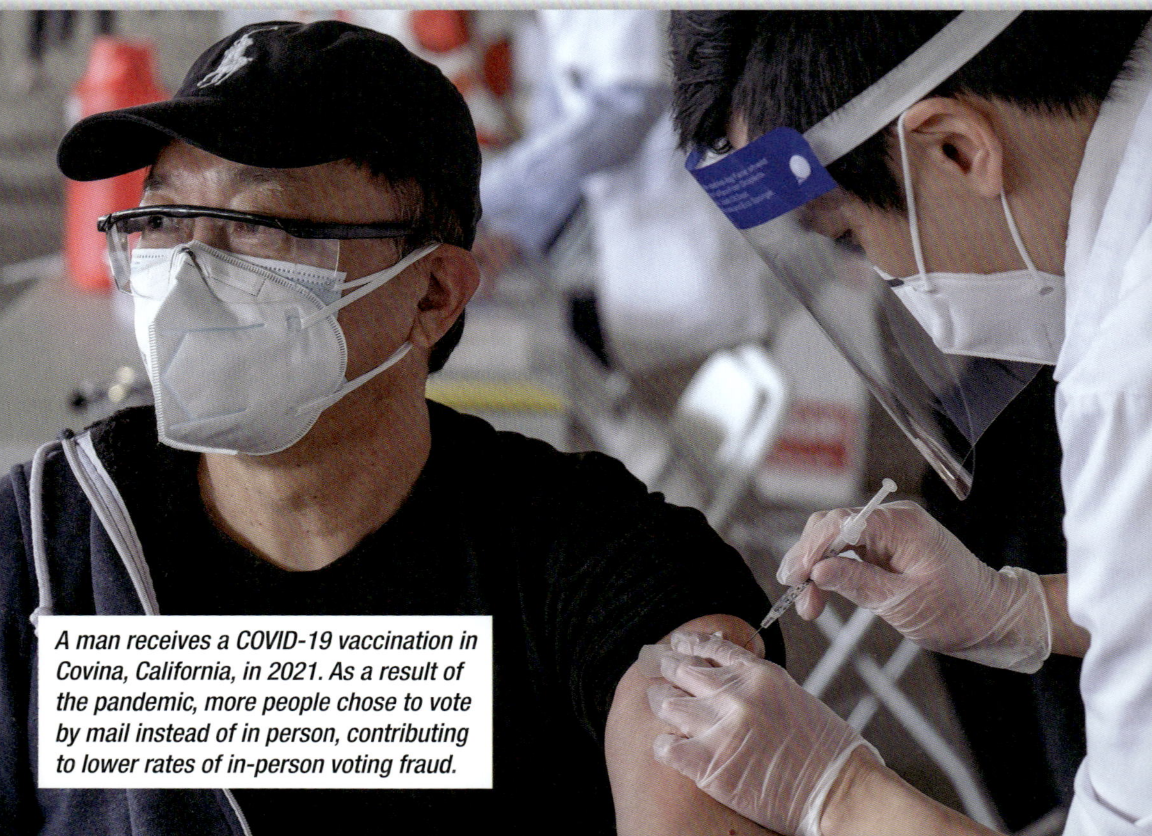

A man receives a COVID-19 vaccination in Covina, California, in 2021. As a result of the pandemic, more people chose to vote by mail instead of in person, contributing to lower rates of in-person voting fraud.

Misinformation About Fake ID Voter Fraud

Many Americans falsely believe that voter impersonation fraud is a widespread problem, and these beliefs have been exacerbated by misinformation on social media. One example of this was a November 2020 Facebook post that read, "Feds Seize 19,888 Fake State Driver Licenses (Made in China) in Chicago O'Hare Airport—ALL Registered to Vote—ALL Democrat!" The claim was that the Chinese government was sending thousands of fake driver's licenses to Democrats so they could cast fake votes. About 3 million people saw this Facebook post. However, the post was untrue. What really happened was that the government did seize an illegal shipment of counterfeit driver's licenses. But most of the licenses had been ordered by underage college students, presumably so they could buy alcohol. Authorities pointed out that the IDs would have been useless for voting purposes. "These are pieces of plastic," explained David Becker, executive director of the Center for Election Innovation and Research. "That's all they are. They do not have matching records in any official database. It's unfathomable to me that this would even be considered remotely plausible."

Quoted in Ali Swenson, "Not Real News: A Look at What Didn't Happen This Week," Associated Press, September 11, 2020. https://apnews.com.

Poll workers check that signature against the signature the voter used to register. This is the same process used to prevent voter registration fraud.

In addition, one of the main safeguards against impersonation is the routine maintenance of voter rolls—as is the case with voter registration fraud. The names of voters who are deceased, have moved out of state or into another district, or who are otherwise ineligible to vote are routinely removed from voter rolls. This prevents impersonators from stealing the identity of someone who used to be on the list. If a person's name is not on the list, that person cannot be impersonated. Although accurate voter rolls do not eliminate the possibility of voter impersonation, they do make impersonation less likely. Another way that updated voter rolls reduce the possibility of impersonation is by providing poll workers with a list of people who are registered to vote in that district—and their addresses. In every state, regardless of the state's voter ID laws, voters have to confirm both their name and address with the poll worker. People who do not know

A poll worker in Massachusetts reviews a paper voter roll in 2022. Voter rolls help prevent impersonation because poll workers use them to keep track of who votes.

the address of the person they are trying to impersonate will not be able to proceed—although this safeguard will not work if the impersonator does know the address.

Voter rolls also help prevent impersonation because poll workers use them to keep track of who votes. If the real voter has already voted, the impersonator will get caught when trying to vote with that person's name. If the impersonator votes first, his or her vote will not count if the real voter shows up to vote and provides additional evidence of his or her identity.

Provisional ballots also protect against voter impersonation fraud. If a poll worker suspects impersonation or otherwise cannot confirm a voter's identity, that person can vote with a provisional ballot. After Election Day, provisional ballots are investigated. This gives officials an opportunity to find any provisional ballots that were cast fraudulently.

In smaller communities another safeguard against election fraud is simply the fact that elections are local. According to the 2020 US Census, although most Americans live in urban areas, about 14 percent of the population lives in rural areas with fewer than twenty-three thousand people in their county. People in these communities are likely to know the people working at their local polling place, since polls nationwide are staffed by multiple people who live in that precinct. When neighbors know each other, it is hard to pretend to be someone else.

Is In-Person Voter Impersonation a Serious Problem?

The majority of Americans support photo voter ID laws, a measure designed to prevent voter impersonation at the polls. However, contrary to what some might think, polling places are not filled with voters sporting flimsy disguises in order to cast a vote in another person's name. Experts say that voter impersonation is the least common form of voter fraud. Safeguards are in place to catch this type of fraud. Despite this, many voters and state legislatures continue to support photo voter ID laws, which may make it more difficult for some Americans to vote.

CHAPTER THREE

Voting Machines

"We have to get rid of all voting machines and save our country!"[17] announced MyPillow chief executive officer Mike Lindell in 2023. After the 2020 election, Lindell had frequently repeated former president Donald Trump's claims that voting machines had been tampered with during the election. In Lindell's 2021 documentary, *Absolute Proof*, he claimed that Dominion Voting Systems manipulated its software so that votes for Trump were deleted and votes for Joe Biden were counted multiple times. He called this "the biggest cover-up for the biggest crime in United States history—probably in world history."[18]

Dominion has categorically denied Lindell's claims. In a statement, the company said, "No credible evidence has ever been presented to any court or authority that voting machines did anything other than count votes accurately and reliably in all states."[19] In February 2023 Dominion sued Lindell for $1.3 million dollars for defamation. Dominion also sued Fox News for defamation after anchors on the network reinforced Trump's negative claims about Dominion voting machines. In April 2023 Fox settled the lawsuit, agreeing to pay Dominion $787.5 million rather than go to trial.

Can the public trust voting machines? Republicans and Democrats disagree about this issue. According to a 2023 AP-NORC poll, only 29 percent of Republicans believe that paper ballots that are scanned into a machine will be counted accurately, as opposed to 63 percent of Democrats.

Most Republicans and Democrats do agree on one point: there are vulnerabilities in voting machine technology that need to be addressed in order to prevent future voting machine fraud, as well as malfunctions. The controversy is whether the machines actually have been tampered with during elections. The federal government's Cybersecurity & Infrastructure Security Agency (CISA) says they have not. In a 2022 investigation of voting machine vulnerabilities, the agency reported, "While these vulnerabilities present risks that should be mitigated as soon as possible, CISA has no evidence that these vulnerabilities have been exploited in any elections."[20]

How Do Voting Machines Work?

Before 2002, voting machines were low-tech. People commonly voted on machines that required voters to pull a lever to select the name of their preferred candidate. Others voted by punching out the name of their preferred candidate on a punch card.

This changed after the 2000 presidential election, which George W. Bush won because of his very narrow win in Florida. Because the election was so close, there was a recount of the punch card ballots in Florida. The recount was heated because many voters had not completely punched holes into their ballots, and there was controversy about how to count these votes. In response to this, low-tech voting systems like lever machines and punch card counting devices were banned in all federal elections.

Today almost all polling places use one of two types of voting machines. The most common type is scanned paper ballot voting, which works similarly to the way that standardized tests are scored. Voters are handed ballots that have circles next to the names of candidates. They fill in the holes with dark ink. In most polling places voters then insert the ballot into a scanner. Later in the day, poll workers run a procedure on the scanner that prints

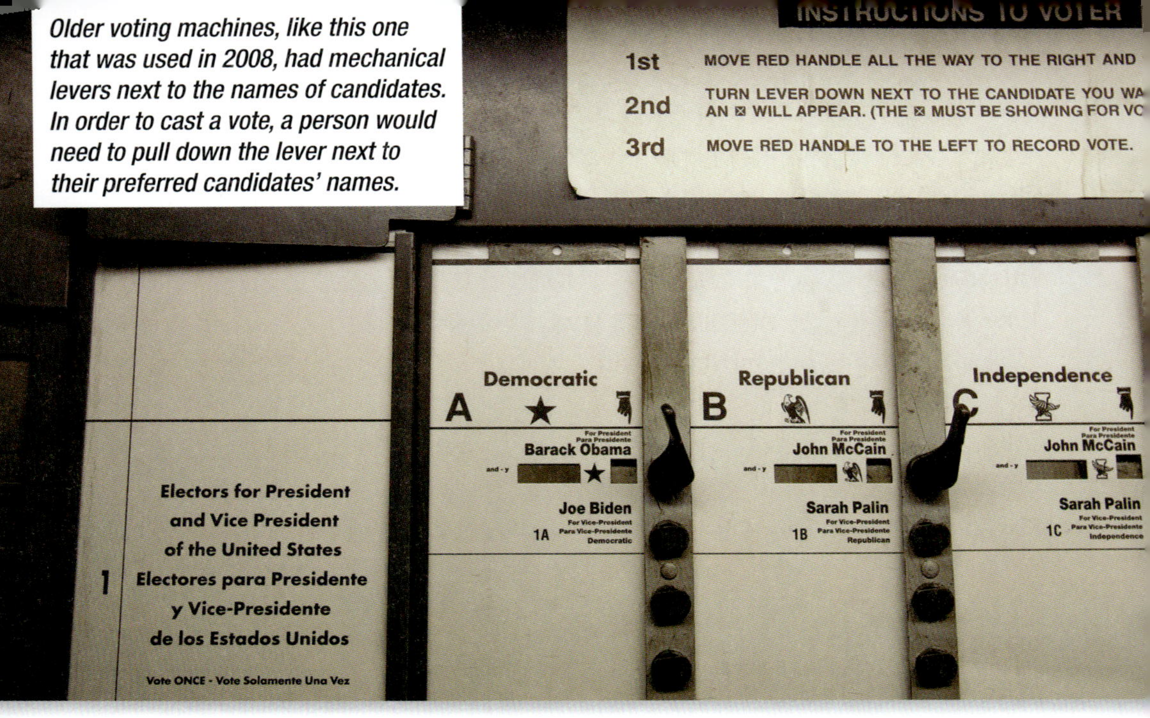

Older voting machines, like this one that was used in 2008, had mechanical levers next to the names of candidates. In order to cast a vote, a person would need to pull down the lever next to their preferred candidates' names.

out the vote totals. In some polling places voters do not scan their ballots: instead, completed ballots are dropped into a box, and the votes are scanned at a central office. Mail-in ballots are also scanned at a central office.

The paper ballots, which never include any information that would identify the voter, are saved so that there is a paper trail. These ballots can be counted by hand in case there is a recount, which happens when there is a very close election. They also can be hand-counted in case of a scanner malfunction.

In some states people vote by using direct-recording electronic (DRE) machines. In DRE voting, people cast their votes directly onto small monitors, usually by pressing the name of the candidates on a touch screen. Most DREs print out a paper record of the voters' choices that they can review before submitting their ballot. These paper records, called voter-verified paper audit trails, can be used in case of a recount or malfunction. In some states voters submit the printed document as their ballot. In other states officials tally the vote total on the DRE machines and send this to the election office.

What Is Voting Machine Tampering?

Voting machine tampering is an attempt by an individual or a group to interfere with the use of equipment that is used to count votes during an election. This includes adding, deleting, changing, or otherwise altering the data that is tabulated by a voting machine. It may also include stealing or damaging election equipment.

Unlike voter registration fraud and voter impersonation, voting machine tampering is almost never the act of an individual voter who is trying to vote illegally. One of the few documented cases of a voter tampering with equipment was that of Richard Patton, a Colorado voter who broke a seal on a voting machine while he was voting and inserted a USB device during the 2022 election. It is unclear why he did this, and a judge dismissed the case after finding Patton mentally incompetent.

Voting machine companies are one type of organization that could potentially tamper with voting machines. After the 2020 election, Donald Trump and his supporters claimed that Dominion Voting Systems altered the results of its machines so that Trump lost and Biden won. "We have testimony of different workers admitting that they were trained how to dispose of Trump votes and add to Biden votes," claimed Trump's lawyer

Hanging Chads and the End of Punch Card Voting

The 2000 presidential election brought an abrupt end to punch card voting in federal elections. Punch cards seem simple enough; voters punch holes on a card that correspond to their preferred candidates. The little bits of the card that get punched out are called chads. It turned out that the election was extremely close. In Florida, Republican George W. Bush earned only 537 votes more than Democrat Al Gore. The outcome of the Florida election was consequential because whoever won Florida would have enough electoral votes to win the election and become president. As with most elections this close, the state conducted a recount. The recount was complicated. Many voters had not punched the chads all the way through the cards, causing what was called a hanging chad, which voting machines did not count. There was a good deal of controversy over how to count these ballots. The decision eventually was made by the US Supreme Court about a month before the inauguration, and Bush became president. In 2002 the Help America Vote Act ended punch card voting in all but small, local elections.

Sidney Powell at a November 19, 2020, press conference. "The software has a feature pursuant to which you can drag and drop any number of batches of votes to the candidate of your choice, or simply throw them away."[21]

Dominion vehemently denied Powell's claims. "Dominion's vote counts have been repeatedly verified by paper ballot recounts and independent audits," the company stated. "Dominion is a non-partisan company that has proudly partnered with public officials from both parties in accurately tabulating the votes of the American people in both 'red' and 'blue' states."[22] After the 2020 election, the CISA investigated voting machines—including Dominion voting machines—to see whether fraud had been committed. The agency concluded, "There is no evidence that any voting system deleted or lost votes, changed votes, or was in any way compromised."[23]

Another group of people who could potentially tamper with voting machines are election officials. Since 2020 the few documented cases of this have been of Trump supporters who stole

A poll worker explains a touch-screen voting machine to a voter. Touch screen machines are common in some states.

voting machines and data for the purpose of investigating these for fraud. For example, in 2022 a Colorado election clerk and her deputy were indicted for making an illegal copy of a voting machine hard drive so that they could search it. Similarly, in 2023 a former Michigan Republican state representative and two lawyers were charged with election fraud for stealing and inspecting the data on voting machines.

Another potential type of voting machine tampering is an attack by hackers. A hacker could potentially modify data or insert malware into the system to damage it. "These vulnerabilities, for the most part, are not ones that could be easily exploited by someone who walks in off the street," says J. Alex Halderman, a computer scientist who conducts research for CISA. However, he warns, "they are things that we should worry could be exploited by sophisticated attackers, such as hostile nation states, or by election insiders, and they would carry very serious consequences."[24]

However, there is no evidence that this kind of fraud has occurred or that it is likely to occur. "We have no evidence that these vulnerabilities have been exploited and no evidence that they have affected any election results," says Brandon Wales, executive director of CISA. "Of note, states' standard election security procedures would detect exploitation of these vulnerabilities and in many cases would prevent attempts entirely. This makes it very unlikely that these vulnerabilities could affect an election."[25]

Existing Safeguards to Secure Voting Machines

Voting machine tampering is rare because of features built into the system to prevent it. For one thing, because elections are decentralized and run by local governments, it is very difficult for someone who is tampering with machines to affect a national election. "It is close to impossible to impact a nationwide election with a technological attack, and change the outcome of an election," explain Major Garrett and David Becker. "It would require a conspiracy of thousands of election officials and others all over the country, without any of them revealing the existence of this extensive conspiracy."[26]

This safeguard is strengthened by the fact that voting machines are not connected to the internet. Garrett and Becker argue, "While no technology is unhackable and impervious to malware, and voting machines are no exception, the lack of connectivity makes it very difficult to infect voting machines in large numbers."[27] Moreover, guidelines of the US Election Assistance Commission, a federal agency that provides resources to local election officials, strongly suggest that wireless technology not be used to transmit voting data, which further diminishes the likelihood of hacking.

In addition, thanks to updates to voting systems from 2016 to 2020, almost all voting machines now have a paper trail. About 95 percent of voting machines are backed up with paper. This makes it easier to conduct postelection tests of the voting equipment to make sure the machines worked properly. It also makes it easier to conduct a recount if necessary. In addition to the paper trail, many scanners and DRE machines are attached to two or more memory devices, which can be checked to make sure they match each other and match the tabulated results.

Although elections are decentralized, states have federal resources to help them prevent voting machine fraud. The US Election Assistance Commission provides local officials with voluntary guidelines for securing, testing, and auditing voting equipment. It also certifies voting systems to make sure they are working correctly. In addition, CISA conducts free cybersecurity vulnerability tests on local voting systems to reduce the possibility of tampering.

Preventing Future Security Problems

To date, voting machine tampering is almost nonexistent. However, Democrats and Republicans agree that there are vulnerabilities

A man tests a voting machine in Milwaukee, Wisconsin, in 2020 after the Trump campaign asked for a recount. Because most machines now have a paper trail, it is easier to do post-election testing and recounting if necessary.

in the system that could lead to tampering, including from foreign adversaries. In its 2022 report, CISA specifically noted some of the vulnerabilities in the Dominion voting system. This includes the possibility that attackers could spread malware into the system or modify code in a way that changes votes. To prevent this, CISA published recommendations that include better physical storage of election equipment, stronger passwords, and rigorous postelection testing to make sure machines were not hacked.

In a 2023 report on election security, Derek Tisler and Lawrence Norden of the Brennan Center for Justice praised this CISA report but argued that CISA needs to better communicate the information in the report to local election officials. They also urged CISA and other government agencies to communicate with local officials about available cybersecurity resources, including CISA's free vulnerability scan. According to Tisler and Norden, "Only 29 percent of local election officials said that they were aware of CISA's cybersecurity vulnerability scan, and just 20 percent of those who were aware availed themselves of this free service."[28]

Tisler and Norden also recommended increased federal spending on election security. They argued, "States need more and consistent funding to upgrade voting machines, add registration systems, hire additional cybersecurity support, and implement thorough postelection audits."[29] They urged states to purchase new voting equipment, since over half of all states use voting equipment that will be at least ten years old by the 2024 election. In addition, they recommended the immediate replacement of the 5 percent of voting machines that do not have a paper trail.

Why We Cannot Vote Online

Americans do so many things online. They pay bills, apply for jobs, and shop for just about everything. So why are people not allowed to vote online? In fact, some countries like Estonia have experimented with online voting. However, cybersecurity experts say that the convenience of online voting is not worth the very real risk of hacking. "The greatest threat to democracy on Election Day is hacking, and cybersecurity experts have long agreed that the intelligent response is to take as much cyber out of the security equation as possible," explains the *Washington Post* editorial board.

As many businesses and government agencies can attest, hacking can lead to all sorts of problems, but some businesses are better able to survive them than others. For example, credit card companies assume that a small percentage of their transactions will be fraudulent, and they consider this an acceptable loss. If a cardholder's credit card number is stolen to make an online purchase, most credit card companies will take the fraudulent charges off the cardholder's bill.

Voting does not work this way. If someone's vote is tampered with online, that vote is simply lost. When it comes to voting, there is no acceptable loss.

Washington Post Editorial Board, "Why Can't We Vote Online? Let Us Count the Ways," *Washington Post*, April 24, 2020. www.washingtonpost.com.

Voting Machines Are Secure but Could Be More Secure

There is no evidence that voting machine tampering has had an impact on elections. In recent years there have been almost no instances of voting machine tampering. Most of the cases that technically fell under the category of tampering were actually election officials who were trying to investigate fraud on their own systems. The claims of rampant voter fraud by individuals like Mike Lindell and Sidney Powell are false. Safeguards within the voting system, like paper trails and decentralized elections, make it very difficult for anyone to hack into the system and cause significant damage. However, vulnerabilities in the system do exist. To prevent voting machine fraud in the future, states need to update their security plans and prioritize spending on new equipment and other technology.

CHAPTER FOUR

Voting by Mail

In 2018 a minister named Mark Harris ran for US Congress in North Carolina's ninth district. He stunned everyone by defeating incumbent representative Robert Pittenger in the Republican primary by fewer than one thousand votes.

However, what looked like a remarkable victory turned out to be a remarkable case of mail-in ballot fraud. In rural Bladen County, a Harris campaign aide named McCrae Dowless had taken advantage of local people who were impoverished and struggling with addiction. He had paid them a few hundred dollars apiece to go door-to-door and commit mail-in ballot fraud. "Witnesses told state officials that Dowless, with the help of his assistants, had gathered hundreds of absentee ballots from Bladen County in 2018," reports Gary D. Robertson of the Associated Press. "Those workers testified they were directed to collect blank or incomplete ballots, forge signatures on them and even fill in votes for local candidates."[30] Election officials investigated the case because of inconsistencies—like hundreds of mail-in ballots being sent in at the same time—and the election results were overturned in favor of Pittenger.

This was a blatant case of mail-in ballot fraud. There have been other documented cases of fraud involving mail-in ballots. In fact, mail-in ballot fraud is more common than other types of voter and election fraud. But how common is it? And how secure is voting by mail? As with many issues today, Americans are divided on these questions. Party affiliation is a clear dividing line. According to a 2022 Pew Research Center poll, only 37 percent of Republicans said they were confident that mail-in votes would be counted accurately in the 2022 election, as opposed to 88 percent of Democrats. This reflects the position of Donald Trump and many of his supporters during the 2020 and 2022 elections that mail-in ballot fraud was rampant. As a result of the Republican Party's campaign against mail-in voting, many states have proposed or passed legislation to limit it. This includes laws that call for shorter windows of time for voters to apply for and send in a mail-in ballot, along with laws that restrict who can receive these ballots.

However, experts agree that although fraud involving mail-in ballots is more common than other kinds of voter fraud, it is not widespread. In fact, in July 2023 the Republican National Committee backed away from the party's earlier stance against voting by mail and urged Republicans to do so in the 2024 election.

How Does Voting by Mail Work?

Voting by mail in the United States—which is sometimes known as absentee voting—began during the Civil War so that soldiers could cast their votes. For many years most Americans who used absentee ballots were living abroad or serving in the military. In the 1970s and 1980s, as society became more mobile, absentee voting became more common. Since the 2010s many states have promoted mail-in voting as a way to increase voter turnout. Voting by mail exploded in popularity in 2020 because of the COVID-19 pandemic, when about 46 percent of voters nationwide mailed in their ballots.

State requirements for who is allowed to vote by mail differ. Some states only allow excuse-required absentee voting, which means that voters need to provide a valid excuse for why they cannot get to the polls on Election Day. This may include illness, disability, or military service. Other states offer no-excuse absentee voting, which means that any registered voter can request an absentee ballot without giving a reason. Some states go further and mail ballots to all registered voters. Voters in these states can choose either to mail in their ballots or vote at a polling place.

States also have different rules for how voters cast and send mail-in ballots. After the voter completes the ballot, the ballot goes into an envelope that is marked with a tracking system like a bar code. The voter signs his or her name on the envelope, which will be stored separately from the ballot so that the voter's choices remain anonymous. In some states voters also need to write down their driver's license number, state ID number, or last four digits of their Social Security number on this envelope. Some states also require voters to have a witness sign this envelope. The ballot envelope goes into a mailing envelope. The voter can mail this, or as an alternative, most states have ballot drop boxes or designated government offices where voters can drop off ballots. States have different deadlines for when mail-in ballots need to be received.

The ballots are delivered to central processing centers. There election officials match the signature on the ballot with the signature on file from when the voter registered. If a state asks for identifying information like a driver's license number, election officials check this as well. Many states require that the ballots be examined by more than one election official. If there is not a match, the ballot is rejected and not counted, and in some states, voters will receive a replacement ballot. Ballots are stored in a secure location until they are counted.

What Is Vote-by-Mail Fraud?

There are a number of potential ways that a mailed ballot can be used fraudulently. For example, an individual can vote with someone else's ballot, which is a form of voter impersonation. Voters might also use a mail-in ballot as an opportunity to vote twice—once at a polling place and once by mail—or might vote by mail in more than one state. In addition, just as it is illegal for noncitizens and some felons to vote at a polling place, it is illegal for them to vote by mail. It is also illegal to create a counterfeit mail-in ballot.

Mail-in ballots need to be filled out privately. At a polling place, it is illegal for someone to stand close enough to a voter to see his or her ballot choices. This is true at home as well. It is also illegal to pressure or force someone to vote a certain way.

Some types of mail-in ballot fraud involve election officials or campaign volunteers. It is illegal for election officials to read, destroy, or intentionally miscount ballots. It is also illegal to intentionally accept mail-in ballots that should not be accepted or reject ballots that should not be rejected. Volunteers or election officials cannot fill in ballots on behalf of voters.

Because states have different laws governing the use of mail-in ballots, some actions are legal in some states but not others. For example, some states allow voters to deliver other people's completed ballots to ballot boxes, and some do not.

How Common Is Vote-by-Mail Fraud?

Hans A. von Spakovsky of the Heritage Foundation argues that mail-in ballots should rarely be used because they are the least

Opponents of mail-in voting argue that elections can be swayed by a practice that is sometimes known as ballot harvesting. This term refers to third parties—often campaign workers—who visit voters at home and offer to mail or deliver their completed ballots. Critics say that this practice leaves way too much room for fraud. Campaign workers could potentially throw away ballots. They also could persuade voters to give them unsealed or incomplete ballots and fill out the ballots themselves—as was the case in the North Carolina congressional election. However, supporters of this practice argue that this is a legitimate way to increase voter turnout. Voters who are elderly, disabled, or working long hours might have trouble getting to a post office or drop box. Whether or not this practice is legal varies by state. Some states place limitations on how many ballots a voter can drop off or mail. This allows people to drop off ballots for others in their household or for an elderly neighbor, for example, but not for large numbers of people. Other states do not impose these kinds of limits.

secure method of voting. "Mail-in or absentee ballots are the ones most susceptible to being stolen, altered, and forged, and to having the voters be pressured or coerced when voting, because they are the only type of ballots marked in an unsupervised, unobserved setting,"[31] he argues.

The Heritage Foundation database contains about 270 examples of mail-in ballot fraud that occurred from 1988 to 2023. Most of the examples are of individual voters using mail-in ballots fraudulently. For example, Tracey McKee of Scottsdale, Arizona, was convicted in 2022 of sending in her deceased mother's ballot, and Richard Fox was convicted in 2023 of voting by mail in both West Virginia and Florida. Only a few cases in the database—like the congressional election case in North Carolina—involved fraud by election officials. For example, in Lawrenceburg, Indiana, two city employees were convicted in 2022 of filling out absentee ballots on behalf of voters.

Election experts acknowledge that mail-in ballots are more susceptible to fraud than other forms of voting. "Absentee voter fraud, while very rare, is much more likely than voter impersonation fraud at a polling place," explains Hasen. "Absentee votes can be bought, stolen, altered, or destroyed outside of the presence of election officials."[32]

Despite these vulnerabilities, fraud involving mail-in ballots does not often occur. Edie Goldenberg, a University of Michigan political scientist who led a study on voter fraud, states, "The evidence we reviewed finds that voting by mail is rarely subject to fraud, does not give an advantage to one political party over another and can in fact inspire public confidence in the voting process, if done properly."[33]

Moreover, after conducting several studies about voting fraud, the Associated Press concluded that fraud involving mail-in ballots almost never occurs. "Claims that mail-in voting has caused widespread voter fraud in the past are unsubstantiated," the As-

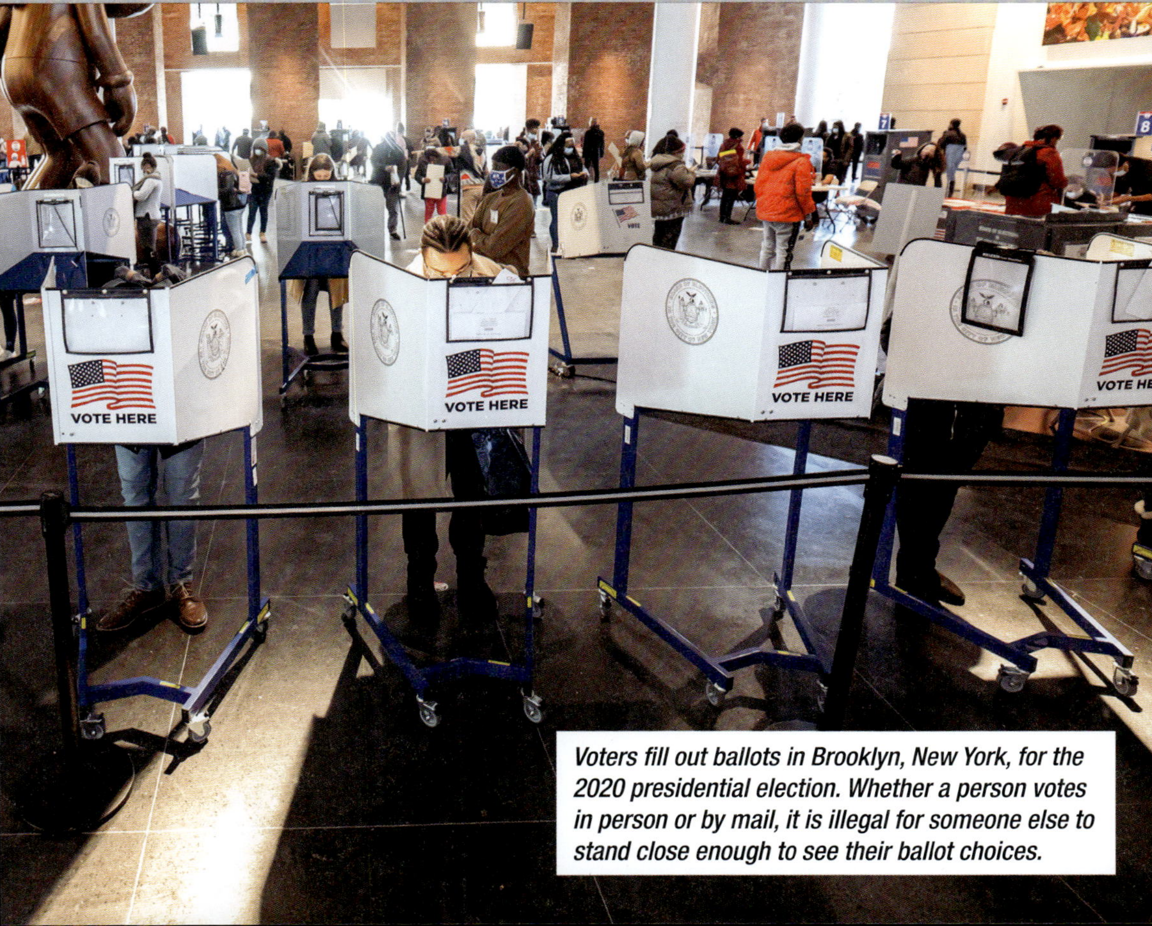

Voters fill out ballots in Brooklyn, New York, for the 2020 presidential election. Whether a person votes in person or by mail, it is illegal for someone else to stand close enough to see their ballot choices.

sociated Press stated in 2022. "Additionally, an [Associated Press] survey of state election officials across the U.S. found that the expanded use of drop boxes during the 2020 race did not lead to cases of fraud, vandalism or theft that could have impacted the results."[34]

Safeguards Against Vote-by-Mail Fraud

Security measures built into the system have helped to prevent mail-in voting fraud. These measures begin when the voter is sent a ballot in the mail. Election officials routinely check to make sure the correct voter is receiving a ballot. "Voter lists are constantly checked against the postal service, motor vehicle department records, and other data to make sure the information is accurate,"[35] explain Major Garrett and David Becker. This verification process greatly reduces the chance that another person will get hold of someone's ballot and attempt to use it fraudulently.

In addition, the US Postal Service also keeps careful track of who is sent a ballot. "Mail ballots are coded on the exterior envelope to enable election officials to verify that only official ballots

New Laws About Mail-In Voting

Since 2020 many states have passed new laws about mail-in voting. Some of these laws make mail-in voting more difficult. According to the Brennan Center for Justice, "Since the 2020 election, 21 states have passed 33 laws restricting mail voting access." For example, Ohio passed a law in 2023 that shortens the amount of time people have both to apply for and send in absentee ballots. Ohio also limited the number of ballot drop boxes to one per county. In both South Dakota and Arkansas, ballot drop boxes were banned in 2023. On the other hand, some states have passed laws that make mail-in voting easier. For example, in 2023 Minnesota moved the deadline for receiving mail-in ballots to 8:00 p.m. on Election Day. In addition, Minnesota employers are required to give workers paid time off from work to vote at any time during the forty-six-day-long absentee voting period.

Jasleen Singh and Sara Carter, "States Have Added Nearly 100 Restrictive Laws Since SCOTUS Gutted the Voting Rights Act 10 Years Ago," Brennan Center for Justice, June 23, 2023. www.brennancenter.org.

A US Postal Service employee collects mail from drop-off boxes in Maricopa, Arizona, in 2023. US Postal Service workers are trained to spot counterfeit ballot envelopes.

are used, and that they know exactly who has received a mail ballot,"[36] explain Garrett and Becker. This makes it very unlikely that a person will receive two ballots in the mail or vote twice.

Another built-in safeguard that prevents people from voting with fake ballots is that ballots are also very difficult to counterfeit. "Ballots feature particular design elements that are difficult to copy," explain political scientists Charlotte Hill and Jake Grumbach. "They are printed on special card stock, with exact page size, color and thickness varying by state, or even county or town."[37] Ballots from different locations also have different slates of local candidates. Voters may not notice who is on the ballot for school board or sewer commissioner at a particular location, but election officials will notice if these candidates are omitted or listed incorrectly on a counterfeit ballot. It is also very difficult to

> "Ballots feature particular design elements that are difficult to copy. They are printed on special card stock, with exact page size, color and thickness varying by state, or even county or town."[37]
>
> —Charlotte Hill and Jake Grumbach, political scientists

duplicate the official envelopes that voters use to send back their ballots. US Postal Service workers are trained to spot counterfeit envelopes, as are the election officials who receive the ballots.

Another built-in safeguard is that election officials have to carefully inspect each ballot before it is accepted. Ballots are not accepted unless they are sealed and the signature on the ballot matches the signature on file from voter registration. In some states multiple election officials inspect each ballot. Election officials also scan the ballot into the system to prevent duplicate voting.

After counting the votes, election officials have to check their work. "The final step is the canvassing process in which election officials must reconcile all their counts, ensuring the number of ballots cast equals the number of voters who voted," explains Christina A. Cassidy of the Associated Press. "Any discrepancies are researched, and election officials provide detailed explanations before the election can be certified."[38] After mail-in ballots are received and accepted, they are stored in secure, locked locations until they are ready to be counted.

Election Security and Vote by Mail

Voting by mail is by definition an activity that cannot be supervised, and consequently, mail-in voting fraud is the most common kind of voting fraud. Despite this, vote-by-mail fraud is still uncommon. Like voter registration fraud and in-person voter impersonation, vote-by-mail fraud is usually committed by individuals rather than by election officials. Safeguards throughout the mail-in voting system make this kind of fraud much less likely.

CHAPTER FIVE

Counting the Votes

The building was surrounded by a 6-foot-tall (1.8 m) spiked metal gate with a chain-link fence. Multiple security guards stood at each entrance. No one could get in without an official key card. Inside, the workers did their jobs in a room protected by bulletproof glass.

Why was this much security needed? The building was the Maricopa County Tabulation and Election Center in Phoenix, Arizona. The workers inside were counting votes from the 2022 election. In 2022 vote counters around the country faced harassment and even death threats by people who believed that vote counters were intentionally miscounting votes in favor of Democratic candidates.

Threats against vote counters originated in 2020 in Georgia, where votes were being recounted after Donald Trump had lost the presidential election. Election workers were accused of throwing away bags full of ballots and sneaking suitcases of fake ballots into election centers. In one case an election technician was accused of tampering with a voting machine when he was actually just servicing it. He received death threats on Twitter. In a well-publicized case, a mother and daughter who were counting votes were filmed exchanging a piece of candy. Trump's lawyer, Rudy Giuliani, claimed that the item they had exchanged was actually a memory stick filled with voter information, which the two women planned to use to alter the vote count. The women, who received hundreds of death threats, sued Giuliani for defamation. In August 2023 a judge ruled in favor of the women.

Giuliani was ordered to pay for the women's legal fees, and to stand trial before a jury to determine how much he owed the women for defaming them.

All of these claims were investigated by Georgia officials and were proved false. "False claims and knowingly false allegations made against these election workers have done tremendous harm," said Georgia secretary of state Brad Raffensperger. Despite threats and baseless allegations, election workers have continued to do their jobs to ensure that voters' ballots are counted promptly and accurately. The people who count votes perform a task that is a crucial part of the democratic process. As Raffensperger states, "Election workers deserve our praise for being on the front lines."[39]

How Are Votes Counted?

To better understand whether vote-counting fraud is a threat, it is helpful to understand how votes are counted. When people vote in person on Election Day, their ballots are counted in several ways. At the end of the day, election officials print out the vote totals from the voting machines that were used to count ballots. The officials then deliver this information to the local election office. In polling places where voters did not scan their ballots into machines, the ballots are delivered to the election office and counted there. Election workers use equipment that quickly scans and tabulates the ballots.

Mail-in ballots are sent to election centers in envelopes that have been signed by the voter. After election workers inspect the envelopes and confirm the identities of the voters, they store the ballots securely until they are ready to be scanned. In some states these votes cannot be opened and counted until Election Day, but other states allow election workers to count them earlier. Early votes are treated similarly. When people vote before Election Day at designated polling places, they place their ballots into signed

Poll workers count absentee ballots in Detroit, Michigan, in 2020. Their job is a crucial part of the democratic process.

envelopes, which are counted by election officials the same way as mail-in ballots.

The process of counting votes does not end on Election Day. In some states the deadline for sending in mail-in ballots is days or weeks after Election Day, especially for people serving in the military overseas. It also takes longer to count provisional ballots. These are ballots that voters are allowed to cast at a polling place when it is unclear whether they can legally vote. These ballots are investigated, and if they are accepted, they are counted.

Sometimes the winner of an election is announced before all the votes are counted. This is done if it is statistically impossible for anyone else to win. Regardless of when the winner is announced, all eligible votes are counted.

How Do Recounts Work?

In a recount, votes are counted again to make sure the final count is accurate. In some states recounts happen automatically in close elections. The rules for this vary by state; for example, in North

Dakota, an automatic recount happens if a candidate loses by one percentage point in the primary or by half a percentage point in the general election. Recounts can also be requested by an individual or political party if they suspect the vote count was inaccurate. Not all recount requests are accepted, and states have rules about how long after the election a recount can be requested.

There are two kinds of recounts. In a machine recount, votes that were scanned into a machine are scanned again to see whether there is a discrepancy in the numbers. These numbers are also compared against the vote totals that were stored in the machine. In a hand recount, workers inspect each ballot carefully before adding it to the count. Hand recounts can be controversial because it is not always clear which candidate a voter intended to choose. This causes time-intensive arguments about individual ballots. Often, states conduct both machine recounts and hand recounts.

Orlando, Florida, election workers prepare ballots for scanning in a voting recount. In a recount, votes are counted again to make sure the final count is accurate.

Why Not Count All Votes by Hand?

Since 2020 some state legislators have proposed doing away with voting machines and instead counting all the votes by hand. They argue that paper ballots are generally more secure than voting machines, which could possibly be hacked. Although voting experts agree that it is important to use ballots as a paper trail in the event of a recount or audit, they strongly disagree that hand counting should replace machine counting. The main problem with hand counting is accuracy. Counting votes is a tedious process that requires a good deal of focus. People counting votes are going to make mistakes that machines do not make. In addition, machine counting is obviously much faster than hand counting. Over 159 million people voted in the 2020 presidential election. Counting all of those votes by hand would have taken weeks. It also would have required hiring and training thousands of temporary workers to count the votes—an expensive and time-consuming process.

During a recount, election officials also inspect the envelopes that contained mail-in ballots and early votes. They may overturn the original decision either to accept or reject a ballot. Provisional ballots are also inspected, and the original decisions to accept or reject these ballots may be overturned as well.

Recounts almost never change the election results. Even when result totals change, they are usually not significant enough to make a difference. For example, in a 2022 Colorado congressional election, incumbent Lauren Boebert received 548 more votes than her opponent. After a recount, Boebert won the election by 546 votes, 2 fewer votes than before the recount.

In the rare event that an election does get overturned by a recount, it is usually a small local election. The last time a statewide election was overturned was the 2008 Senate race in Minnesota. Democrat Al Franken initially lost to Republican Norm Coleman by 218 votes, but after a recount, Franken won by 225 votes.

What Is Ballot Count Fraud?

Any attempt by a vote counter or election official to deliberately change the final count of an election is fraud. Vote counters could potentially commit fraud in a number of ways, either on Election Day or during a recount. They could remove or dispose of ballots, perhaps because these ballots come from a neighborhood where their candidate is not widely supported. They could run ballots through a machine more than once. They also could modify the votes on a ballot or tamper with ballots so that they cannot be scanned. If a voter did not cast a vote for a school board member and left this blank, an election worker potentially could fill in a vote for them.

Voter count fraud can also happen as officials are making judgments about whether to accept or reject mail-in ballots or provisional ballots. Officials are required to carefully follow the law when making these decisions. Sometimes these decisions are difficult to make, and it is not fraud if an election official makes a poor choice. However, if an election official deliberately rejects ballots that should not be rejected or accepts ballots that should not be accepted, that is fraud.

How Common Is Ballot Count Fraud?

In the ten years from 2013 to 2023, the Heritage Foundation documented six cases of someone attempting to alter the vote count. Three of these were cases in which election workers modified ballots, and one was a case in which an election official stole a ballot box. One of the cases was a scheme by a former Penn-

The Sharpie Controversy

During the 2020 election, many conspiracies spread across social media about the election being rigged in favor of Joe Biden. One such rumor started in Arizona about the use of Sharpies—a brand of permanent marker—to mark ballots. At some polling places, voters were handed Sharpies to mark their ballots, instead of other kinds of black pens. Some voters noticed that the Sharpie ink bled a little bit so some marks could be seen on the other side of the ballot. A rumor quickly spread across social media that ballots with Sharpie bleed could not be read by the scanners and that poll workers were intentionally handing out Sharpies to Republican voters to invalidate their votes. Maricopa County officials quickly explained that ballots marked with Sharpies were read by voting scanners just like all the other ballots. However, the Sharpie rumor fueled the already skyrocketing level of distrust by some Arizona Republicans in the integrity of the election.

sylvania representative who attempted to bribe election judges to falsify election totals in favor of Democratic candidates.

The other case listed in the Heritage Foundation database involved Kathy Funk, an election supervisor who ran for county clerk in Michigan during the 2020 election. She won by seventy-nine votes and anticipated there would be a recount. To help her chances, Funk broke the seal on a container of ballots, which invalidated those ballots so they could not be recounted. She then fabricated a story about how someone had broken in and tampered with the ballot container. In 2022 Funk was sentenced to six months of house arrest and two years of probation.

Mistakes are sometimes made when counting votes, but these are almost always because of human errors and not fraud. These errors almost never impact election outcomes because close elections usually are recounted. For example, a 2023 investigation uncovered votes that were accidentally overcounted in Fulton County, Georgia, during the 2020 election. However, this did not come close to impacting the election outcome, as the investigation discovered 345 votes for Trump in a county where Biden won by about 243,000 votes. Ben Adida, executive director of the election technology company VotingWorks, explains that there was nothing suspicious about finding a small percentage of counting errors in Georgia as the entire state went through two recounts in 2020. "It's not surprising that some mistakes were made in the process of counting more than 5 million ballots,"[40] argues Adida.

Safeguards Against Vote Counting Fraud

Safeguards are built into the system to prevent vote counting fraud. Many of these security measures relate to the protection of the ballots themselves, along with the voting equipment that contains information about the ballots.

Election workers are trained to handle completed ballots in a manner similar to the handling of classified documents. This is called chain of custody, which CISA describes as "a process used to track the movement and control of an asset through its lifecycle by documenting each person and organization who handles an asset, the date/time it was collected or transferred, and the purpose of the transfer."[41] Every time ballots or voting equipment is moved, poll workers are required to log where and why these were moved and who was involved with the transfer.

An important feature of the chain of custody is that no one is ever alone with the ballots or elections equipment. These are always handled by at least two people. Often, it is required that these two people are representatives of different political parties.

The chain of custody also accounts for the storage of ballots and election equipment. Ballots need to be stored in case there is an audit or recount, and mail-in and early votes need to be stored before they are counted. It is crucial that the process of securing this information is carefully documented. As CISA explains, "Many

In 2022, election observers in Reno, Nevada, use binoculars to watch votes being processed from behind the glass. One built-in security feature of the voting process is that much of it happens in front of the public.

state, local, and territorial jurisdictions require specific security protocols for stored ballots and other election records, such as storage in a secure vault featuring double lock systems that can only be opened when authorized representatives from both political parties are present."[42]

Another safeguard against vote tampering is that many voting machines have been updated in recent years. Because 95 percent of voting machines now have a paper trail, it is much easier to conduct postelection audits and recounts to ensure accuracy. In addition, most voting machines store data on multiple memory devices, which makes it easy to spot inconsistencies. "Each tabulator has multiple redundant memory devices, and each is checked to make sure they match," explain Garrett and Becker. "Each also usually prints a hard copy of the tallies in each machine, so those also can be checked and double-checked against the other media on which the counts are stored."[43]

In addition, a built-in security feature of the voting process is that much of it happens in front of the public. According to the US Election Assistance Commission, "Voting equipment testing, election night tabulation, official canvass, audits, and recounts are frequently open to public observation. Observe and see for yourself how election officials safeguard the voting process and verify the integrity of election results."[44]

Election Security and Counting the Votes

Despite widespread claims during the 2020 and 2022 elections that vote counters and election officials were tampering with ballots, this kind of voter fraud almost never happens. There are only a handful of documented cases of people intentionally miscounting or tampering with votes. The system has built-in safeguards to prevent this type of fraud. This includes a chain of custody that ensures that ballots and election equipment are secure.

Introduction: A Real but Rare Problem

1. Quoted in WSB-TV, "Georgia Man Convicted After Stealing Woman's Ballot, Submitting Vote Twice, Officials Say," December 10, 2022. www.wsbtv.com.
2. Quoted in Christina A. Cassidy, "Far Too Little Vote Fraud to Tip Election to Trump, AP Finds," Associated Press, December 14, 2021. https://apnews.com.
3. Katie Samalis-Aldrich and Hans A. von Spakovsky, "Voter Fraud Cases Continue to Occur, Putting Fair and Free Elections in Jeopardy," Heritage Foundation, August 29, 2022. www.heritage.org.
4. Quoted in Tom Vanden Brook and Jeffrey Schweers, "How States Prevent Election Fraud: Time to Count Votes 'Is Not a Sign of Misconduct or Chaos,'" *USA Today*, November 10, 2020. www.usatoday.com.
5. Quoted in Cassidy, "Far Too Little Vote Fraud to Tip Election to Trump, AP Finds."

Chapter One: Registering to Vote

6. Quoted in Brandon Girod, "DeSantis Inks Law Giving Him 'All-Clear' to Run for President. Here's What Else Is Inside," *Pensacola (FL) News Journal*, May 23, 2023. www.pnj.com.
7. Quoted in Rachel Janfaza, "Voter Registration, Explained," CNN, September 22, 2020. www.cnn.com.
8. Cassidy, "Far Too Little Voter Fraud to Tip Election to Trump, AP Finds."
9. Lawrence Mower, "Police Cameras Show Confusion, Anger over DeSantis' Voter Fraud Arrests," *Tampa Bay (FL) Times*, October 18, 2022. www.tampabay.com.
10. Major Garrett and David Becker, *The Big Truth: Upholding Democracy in the Age of the Big Lie*. New York: Diversion, 2022, p. 73.
11. Quoted in Caltech Science Exchange, "How Do Election Officials Check for and Prevent Voter Registration Fraud?," 2023. https://scienceexchange.caltech.edu.

Chapter Two: In-Person Voter Impersonation

12. J. Christian Adams, "Voter ID Laws: Do We Need Them? Pro," *Northwest Arkansas Democrat Gazette*, February 2, 2020. www.nwaonline.com.

13. American Civil Liberties Union, "Fact Sheet on Voter ID Laws," 2021. www.aclu.org.

14. American Civil Liberties Union, "Fact Sheet on Voter ID Laws."

15. League of Women Voters, "What's So Bad About Voter ID Laws?," May 23, 2023. www.lwv.org.

16. Richard Hasen, *Election Meltdown: Dirty Tricks, Distrust, and the Threat to American Democracy*. New Haven, CT: Yale University Press, 2020, p. 21.

Chapter Three: Voting Machines

17. Mike Lindell (@realMikeLindell), "We have to get rid of all the voting machines and save our country," Twitter, February 3, 2023, 5:28 p.m. https://twitter.com/realMikeLindell/status/1621651835760132101.

18. Quoted in Stuart A. Thompson, "Attacks on Dominion Voting Persist Despite High-Profile Lawsuits," *New York Times*, April 7, 2023. www.nytimes.com.

19. Quoted in Thompson, "Attacks on Dominion Voting Persist Despite High-Profile Lawsuits."

20. Cybersecurity & Infrastructure Security Agency. "Vulnerabilities Affecting Dominion Voting Systems ImageCast X," June 3, 2022. www.cisa.gov.

21. Quoted in Rev Transcription Service, "Rudy Giuliani Trump Campaign Press Conference Transcript November 19: Election Fraud Claims," November 19, 2020. www.rev.com.

22. Dominion Voting Systems, "Demand Letter to Sidney Powell," December 16, 2020. www.dominionvoting.com/download/demand-letter-to-sidney-powell-2/?wpdmdl=68273&masterkey=60245c8c809e3.

23. Cybersecurity & Infrastructure Security Agency, "Joint Statement from Elections Infrastructure Government Coordinating Council & the Election Infrastructure Sector Coordinating Executive Committees," November 20, 2020. www.cisa.gov.

24. Quoted in Kate Brumback and Associated Press, "Voting Software in Some States Is Vulnerable to Hacking, U.S. Cyber Agency Says," *Fortune*, May 31, 2022. www.fortune.com.

25. Quoted in Ellen Nakashima and Amy Gardner, "No Evidence of Exploitation of Dominion Voting Machine Flaws, CISA Finds," *Washington Post*, May 28, 2022. www.washingtonpost.com.

26. Garrett and Becker, *The Big Truth*, p. 117.

27. Garrett and Becker, *The Big Truth*, p. 116.

28. Derek Tisler and Lawrence Norden, *Securing the 2024 Election: Recommendations for Federal, State, and Local Officials*. New York: Brennan Center for Justice, 2023, p. 24.

29. Tisler and Norden, *Securing the 2024 Election*, p. 22.

Chapter Four: Voting by Mail

30. Gary D. Robertson, "Dowless, Key Figure in NC Absentee Ballot Fraud Probe, Dies," Associated Press, April 24, 2022. https://apnews.com.

31. Hans A. von Spakovsky, "We Shouldn't Be Promoting Voting by Mail," Heritage Foundation, December 6, 2022. www.heritage.org.

32. Hasen, *Election Meltdown*, p. 96.

33. Quoted in Howard Manly and Matt Williams, "Should You Vote Early in the 2022 Midterm Elections? 3 Essential Reads," The Conversation, September 13, 2022. www.theconversation.com.

34. Associated Press, "Large Numbers of Mailed Ballots Not Evidence of Election Fraud," November 29, 2022. https://apnews.com.

35. Garrett and Becker, *The Big Truth*, p. 102.

36. Garrett and Becker, *The Big Truth*, p. 102.

37. Charlotte Hill and Jake Grumbach, "6 Ways Mail-In Ballots Are Protected from Fraud," The Conversation, September 17, 2020. www.theconversation.com.

38. Cassidy, "Far Too Little Voter Fraud to Tip Election to Trump, AP Finds."

Chapter Five: Counting the Votes

39. Quoted in Office of the Georgia Secretary of State, "State Election Board Clears Fulton County 'Ballot Suitcase' Investigation; Report Finds No Evidence of Conspiracy, No Fraud," June 20, 2023. https://sos.ga.gov.

40. Quoted in Mark Niesse, "Georgia Investigation Finds Errors in Fulton Audit of 2020 Election," *Atlanta Journal-Constitution*, July 17, 2023. www.ajc.com.

41. Cybersecurity & Infrastructure Security Agency, "Chain of Custody of Critical Infrastructure Systems." www.cisa.gov.

42. Cybersecurity & Infrastructure Security Agency, "Election Security Rumor vs. Reality," 2022. www.cisa.gov.

43. Garrett and Becker, *The Big Truth*, p. 73.

44. US Election Assistance Commission, "Voting Systems Security Measures," October 20, 2022. www.eac.gov.

Election Fraud Database, Heritage Foundation

www.heritage.org/voterfraud

The Heritage Foundation is a conservative think tank, and one of its primary goals is to increase the public's awareness of voter fraud. Its searchable Election Fraud Database contains about fourteen hundred documented instances of voter and election fraud that occurred from 1982 to 2023.

Rock the Vote

https://rockthevote.org

Rock the Vote is an organization that encourages young people to vote and become more politically active. Its website contains information about ways that young people can volunteer for voter turnout efforts.

Vote 411

www.vote411.com

Sponsored by the League of Women Voters Education Fund, Vote 411 is a nonpartisan source of information for voters, including specific information about how to register to vote in all fifty states. Its website offers information about candidates and ballot measures at different voting locations, including links to debate videos.

Voting Rights Project, American Civil Liberties Union

www.aclu.org/issues/voting-rights

The American Civil Liberties Unition provides information about the civil rights of Americans and fights legal battles on behalf of people whose rights have been violated. Much of its work is devoted to defending voting rights. Its Voting Rights Project website provides information about recent voting rights legislation.

When We All Vote

https://whenweallvote.org

Created by former First Lady Michelle Obama, When We All Vote is an organization designed to increase voter turnout, and especially to encourage younger people and people of color to vote. Its website has information about voting rights and voter suppression, as well as instructions on how to register to vote.

Books

Mark Bowden and Matthew Teague, *The Steal: The Attempt to Overturn the 2020 Election and the People Who Stopped It*. New York: Atlantic Monthly, 2022.

Gilda R. Daniels, *Uncounted: The Crisis of Voter Suppression in America*. New York: New York University Press, 2020.

Jeff Fleischer, *Votes of Confidence: A Young Person's Guide to American Elections*. 2nd ed. Minneapolis, MN: Zest, 2020.

Major Garrett and David Becker, *The Big Truth: Upholding Democracy in the Age of the Big Lie*. New York: Diversion, 2022.

Richard Hasen, *Election Meltdown: Dirty Tricks, Distrust, and the Threat to American Democracy*. New Haven, CT: Yale University Press, 2020.

Beto O'Rourke, *We've Got to Try: How the Fight for Voting Rights Makes Everything Else Possible*. New York: Flatiron, 2022.

Brad Raffensperger, *Integrity Counts*. Brentwood, TN: Forefront, 2021.

Erin Geiger Smith, *Thank You for Voting: The Maddening, Enlightening, Inspiring, Truth About Voting in America*. New York: Harper Paperbacks, 2021.

Internet Sources

Christina A. Cassidy, "Far Too Little Voter Fraud to Tip Election to Trump, AP Finds," Associated Press, December 14, 2021. https://apnews.com.

Cybersecurity & Infrastructure Security Agency, "Election Security Rumor vs. Reality," 2022. www.cisa.gov.

Cybersecurity & Infrastructure Security Agency, "Vulnerabilities Affecting Dominion Voting Systems ImageCast X," June 3, 2022. www.cisa.gov.

Rachel Janfaza, "Voter Registration, Explained," CNN, September 22, 2020. www.cnn.com.

Shawna Mizells, "Lawmakers in 32 States Have Introduced Bills to Restrict Voting So Far This Legislative Session," CNN, February 22, 2023. www.cnn.com.

Derek Tisler and Lawrence Norden, *Securing the 2024 Election: Recommendations for Federal, State, and Local Officials*. New York: Brennan Center for Justice, 2023. www.scribd.com.

US Election Assistance Commission, "Election Security," October 22, 2022. www.eac.gov.

INDEX

ABOUT THE AUTHOR

Naomi Rockler is an educational freelance writer who writes non-fiction and fiction books for teenagers. She lives in Minnesota with her husband and daughter.